PETER the Skeeter

Down in the south, where the
moon shines bright,

Halloween fills the air with
a magical light.

Trick-or-treaters dress up on this spooky night!

Buzzing past pumpkins with big glowing grins

There's one little bug that wants to join in.

Dressed up in a costume,

ready to trick-or-treat...

Peter the skeeter wants a friend to meet!

"Mmmmm" grunted Frank.
Oh no! Better run!

After getting wrapped up,
Peter won't do that again!

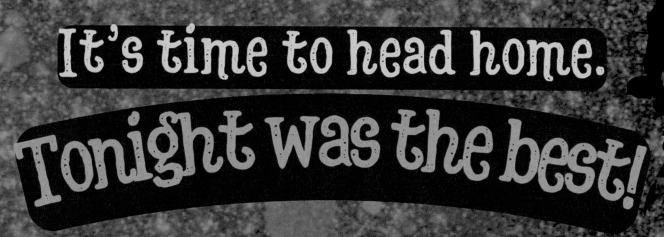

It's time to head home.

Tonight was the best!

With a bag full of candy,
it's now time for rest.

After a whole night of searching,
Peter couldn't find a friend.

Don't worry!
In the morning,
He'll be back at it again!

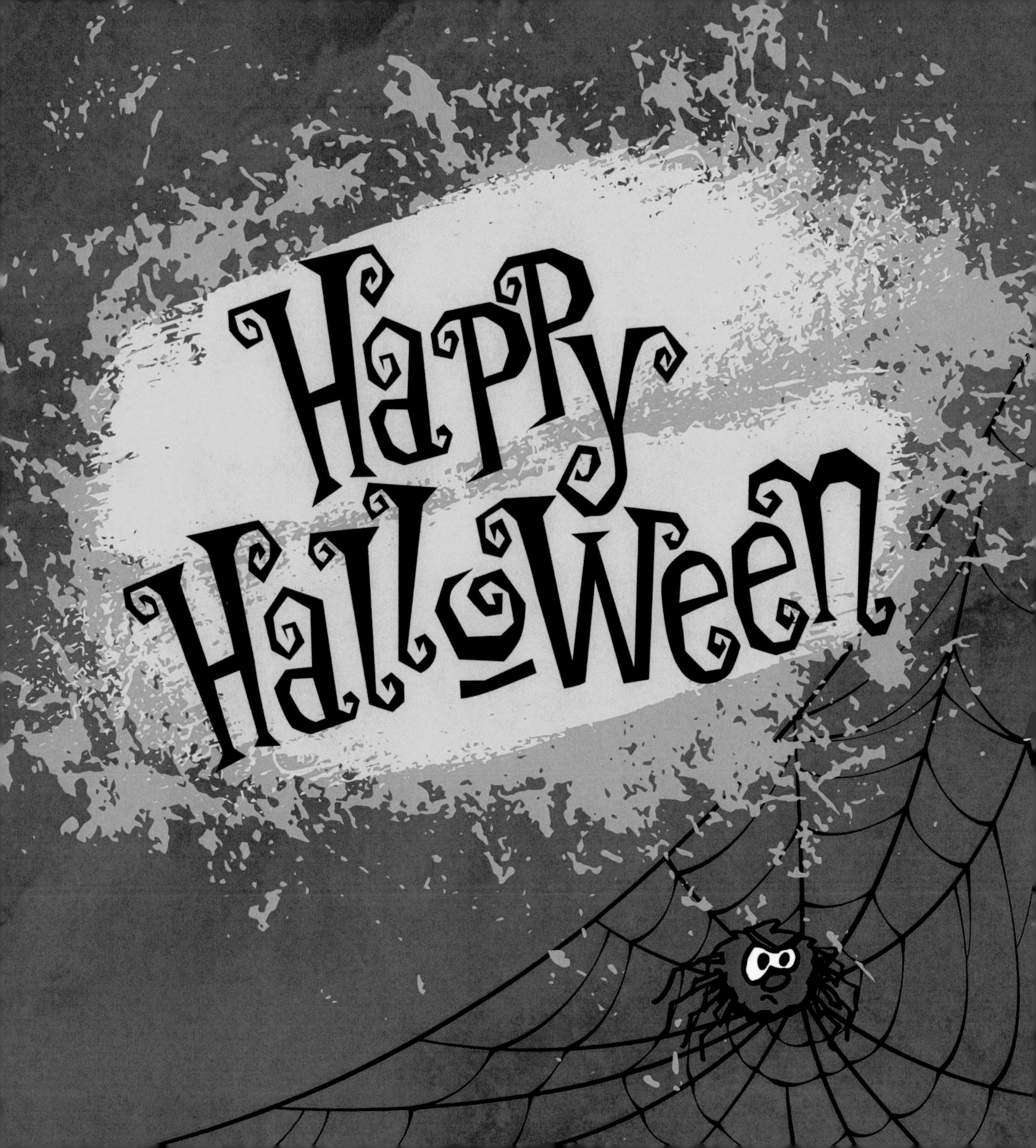
Happy Halloween

Made in the USA
Las Vegas, NV
14 October 2023